I Believe in Santa Claus

by Elizabeth Van Ness

For Sarah and Caroline

THE NIGHT BEFORE
CHRISTMAS

Joyeux Noël *Joyeux Noël*

Joyeux Noël

In this one
neighborhood,
alone...

The gifts would
crush a sled ...

And our
chimney?
Isn't big enough!
(for someone's
head!)

Happy Holidays
Room 29

Merry Christmas

How could
anyone
discover...

Thank you,
Parent Volunteers!

Merry Christmas

What we
wish for
most ...

Make it...

WE WILL SHIP FOR SANTA!

Happy Holidays!
S. Claus

Pack it...

and deliver,
quickly...

Coast to Coast?

Yes, it seems
impossible –

the things he's said to do...

FOR SANTA

But in this world,
we often learn

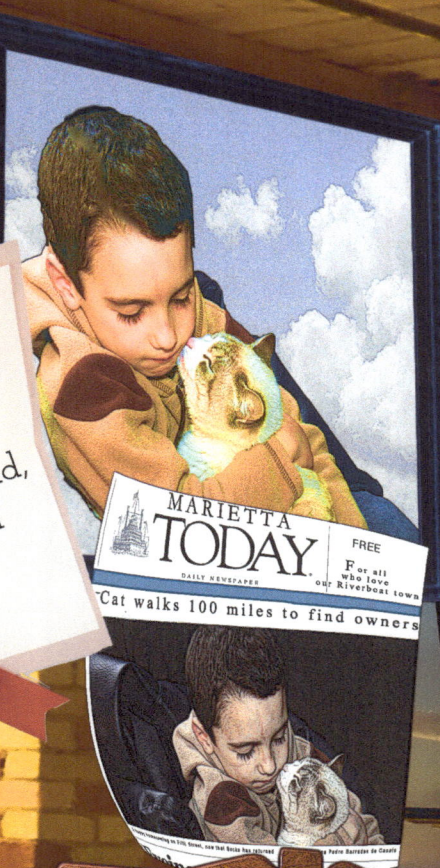

GIRLRADIO.NET
WE BROADCAST GOOD NEWS
On the moon
after perfect
touchdown
Times
JOYFUL REUNION
Sisters find
each other
after 60 years
Is There a Santa Claus?
that
miracles
are
true!
SUNDAY -
Tableau shot - creche,
menorah, koran
(for interfaith peace
event)

And something else,
closer to home,
that he
reminds us of –

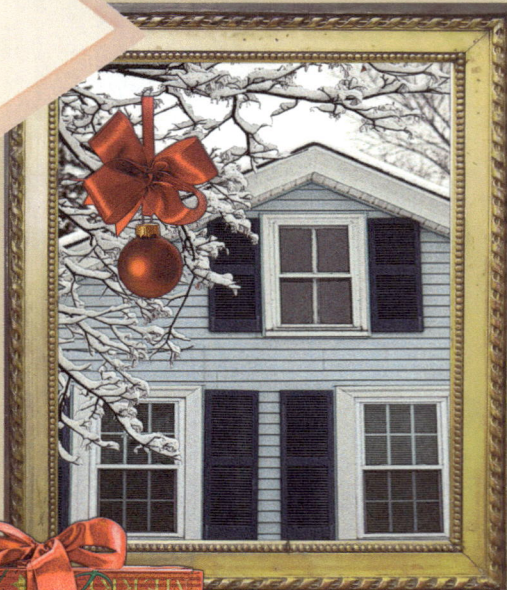

The magic
Christmas
brings our way -
It fills the world
with Love!

Love makes sleighbells
sound like music,
far far away

Love
makes a
cold night
warmer,
in a
wonderful way

Love
makes
snowflakes
taste like
ice cream -
just right!

Love wraps
your wishes
up, like
someone
holding you tight

why
are
we
here?

where
are
we
going

Ancient History
English Literature
The History of Music
HUMAN BIOLOGY
MODERN POLITICS
PHOTOGRAPHY
Chemistry
ENGLISH DICTIONARY
BOOK OF KNOWLEDGE
ADVANCED MATHEMATICS
SOCIOLOGY
LAW
RELIGION • ART
MEDICINE
PHYSICS
WORLD HISTORY

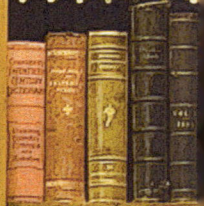

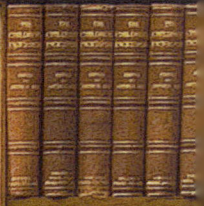

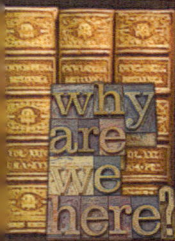

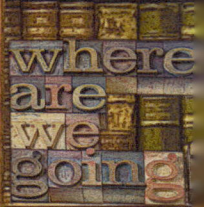

I don't know
all the answers,
but
I'll tell you
what I feel...

I think
Santa Claus is love,
And I KNOW
love is real.

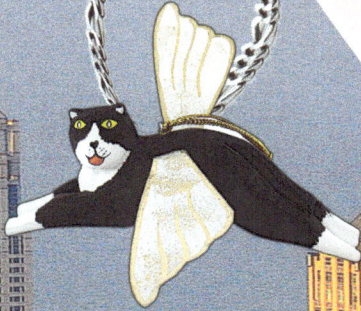

So put aside
those questions,
they are not
worth thinking of.

We
believe in
Santa,
because
we believe in love

TODAY'S EVENTS
*Party for Djibouti group 3pm
*Gingerbread workshop 2pm in cafeteria
*Holiday cards/digital photos – computer lab
*See sched. for Nutcracker, pageant, orch. & choir rehears.
HAPPY HOLIDAYS!!!!!

DONATION BOX

And I believe
that Santa will
make
Christmas
bright
for you...

For
Santa Claus
is
really
love...

And
love
makes
dreams
come
true!

Vicki
and
Santa
Ted

Emily

Shelley

Sharel

Sue

Acknowledgements

Illustrations are derived from photographs
from the author's personal collection, the
National Aeronautics and Space Administration, and
www.shutterstock.com. Information about images licensed
from shutterstock.com is available at www.girlradio.net/santa
A portion of all proceeds from the sale of this book will support
organizations working with children and the arts, including
The Children's Partnership, UCLA's Design for Sharing,
The Institute for Learning, Access and Training
at the Chicago Symphony Orchestra,
and the Santa Monica-Malibu Education Foundation.

Tim

Bill

Jeff

Holly

Line

Special thanks to
family, friends, role
models, mentors and
supporters!

Caro

Barb

Kathy

Kate

Joe

Judy

Bun

Nats

Mom and
Dad

John
and
Jennifer

www.ingramcontent.com/pod-product-compliance
Lightning Source LLC
Chambersburg PA
CBHW042231050426
42443CB00031B/19